Hildegard of Bingen and Her Vision of the Feminine

by Nancy Fierro

Credits

Graphics Layout
Sr. Cecile T. Beresford, CSJ

Cover Design
Sr. Therese Denham, CSJ

Illustrator
Sr. Madeleva Williams, CSJ

Proofreaders
Dr. Anne Eggebroten
Sr. Constance Fitzgerald, CSJ
Stephen M. Fry
Michelle Best

Sheed & Ward™ is a service of The National Catholic Reporter Publishing Company.

ISBN 1-55612-753-7

Published by:
Sheed & Ward
115 E. Armour Blvd. P.O. Box 419492
Kansas City, MO 64141-6492
To order, call: (800) 333-7373

HILDEGARD COMES
TO US TODAY
BECAUSE

WE
NEED
HER
-FIERRO

Foreword

During a question-and-answer session at a recent lecture in Los Angeles, historian Gerda Lerner was asked to name ten or more women who should be well-known but have been left out of mainstream history. One of the first women she named was Hildegard of Bingen, the twelfth-century abbess.

Along with St. Augustine in the fourth century and Martin Luther in the Reformation, Hildegard was a powerful leader not only in her own century but in impact of her ideas on future centuries. In fact, her works are back in print today in numerous translations because of the richness they offer to a world wrung dry by reason, technology, and male dominance. Hildegard gives us a sense of God's intimate presence — not a male God of punishment but a Divine Feminine in whom we on earth live and move like a baby in a cosmic womb.

Dr. Nancy Fierro, a member of Mount St. Mary's College music faculty, has studied Hildegard's music, read her works, and shares in her commitment to life as a woman religious. A professional speaker as well, Nancy gives lively and witty lectures on Hildegard which include excerpts of Hildegard's music and slides of her art. In order to make knowledge of Hildegard accessible to a wider audience, Nancy has distilled from her lectures this brief introduction of Hildegard's life and accomplishments. By reading it, twentieth-century women and men can regain part of the heritage that should have been given to them as they grew up. For those who want to learn more about Hildegard and the Divine Feminine, names of other books and audiotapes are provided.

As a colleague of Dr. Fierro, with a specialization in medieval literature and women's studies, I am delighted to share in introducing you to Hildegard of Bingen. For women today her life and achievements have special relevance. In *The Creation of Feminist Consciousness*, Lerner sums up Hildegard's significance to us: "The life of Hildegard of Bingen exemplifies the breakthrough of a female genius who managed to create an entirely new role for herself and other women without ostensibly violating the patriarchal confines within which she functions." I invite you to read this monograph and expand your own sense of who you are and what you can be.

Dr. Anne Eggebroten
Department of English
Mount St. Mary's College
Los Angeles, California

WHEN ONE'S THOUGHTS ARE...HARMONIOUS THEY HABITUALLY RENDER PHYSICAL CALM AND DEEP INSIGHT

Contents

Foreword   4

Introduction   9

Chronological Clock of Hildegard's Life   10

Early Life   12

Leadership and Visions   14

Creativity and Medicine   20

Hildegard's Music   23

Theology: The Feminine Divine   25

Mary, Ecclesia and Eve   29

Woman's Cloud Nature and Sexuality   32

Creative Authority through the Feminine Divine   36

Last Years   38

Epilogue   40

Endnotes   42

Annotated Bibliography   44

Selected Discography   46

EVERYTHING THAT IS IN HEAVEN ON THE EARTH AND UNDER THE EARTH IS PENETRATED WITH CONNECTEDNESS WITH RELATEDNESS.

Introduction

Hildegard of Bingen was an extraordinarily gifted woman who became a shining star in the spiritual and intellectual world of the twelfth century. Her dazzling creativity extended into the worlds of cosmology, natural science, theology, art, music and medicine. Not only did she believe vehemently in her own capacity to create but she frequently associated creativity with women. She felt that women were endowed with "greening power" — that vitality and fertility inherent in all of fruit-bearing, flower-yielding nature. She also believed that if feminine soul-life was restricted or repressed, all of life would be affected and eventually run dry.

Hildegard gave us powerful gifts not only in her works but in the way she lived her life. Her daring career and her vision of the feminine encompassed a role for women that exceeded the limits of her day and perhaps even of our day. Hildegard's life with its fullness of expression can be a prototype for the conscious feminine image emerging with more clear focus in this century — an image with the power to change life's direction and meaning.[1]

For this reason, I would like to share with you Hildegard's story, her accomplishments and thoughts, with a special attention to her message for women. My hope is that you will be touched by her courageous, creative life.

In preparing this monograph, I relied on English translations of Hildegard's works and English commentaries of her writings. I am especially indebted to Hildegard scholars, Barbara Newman and Sabina Flanagan, for information on Hildegard's theology and concrete details of her life. Having read extensively on Hildegard, I found that many concepts became integrated into my own thinking or have become common knowledge in many sources. I have made reasonable effort to credit specific ideas which are not my own wherever they can be found.

Dr. Nancy Fierro

The Seven Periods of

First Period: 1098 - 1113
Hildegard the Child
- Born as the tenth child to a noble family in Germany
- As a child she experiences spiritual and psychic phemomena
- Given to the Church at age eight
- Apprenticed to the anchoress Jutta
- Embarrassed about her visions, she keeps silence about them

Second Period: 1113 - 1136
Hildegard the Benedictine Nun
- The Anchorage becomes a Benedictine community of nuns
- Between ages 15-18, Hildegard takes vows as a Benedictine nun
- She confides in Jutta concerning her visions

Third Period: 1136 - 1141
Hildegard the Administrator
- Jutta dies
- Hildegard is appointed *Magistra* of the convent
- Abbot Kuno and the Archbishop of Mainz learn of her visions

Fourth Period: 1141 - 1150
Hildegard the Visionary
- Hildegard is ill and depressed
- Hildegard's Awakening — visions of the "Living Light"
- Begins writing first book *Scivias*
- Writes to Abbot Bernard for advice and support
- Pope Eugenius approves Hildegard's work
- Hildegard begins writing down her musical compositions
- Begins correspondence with a wide spectrum of people

Fifth Period: 1150 - 1159
Hildegard the Abbess
- Hildegard falls seriously ill
- Recovers miraculously and founds her own abbey at Rupertsberg
- Gains financial independence and her authority increases
- Completes *Scivias* and begins *Book of Life's Merits*
- Supervises illuminations of her manuscripts
- Writes scientific and medical works
- Hildegard's *protégé*, Sister Rikkarda, dies

Hildegard's Life Journey

Sixth Period: 1159 - 1167
Hildegard, Sibyl of the Rhine

- Travels along the Rhine on her first preaching tour
- Begins writing *Book of Divine Works*
- Gives second and third preaching tours
- Her sermons are copied and disseminated

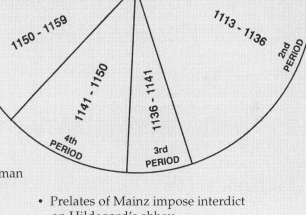

PERIOD 7th

1167 - 1179

PERIOD 1st

1098 - 1113

6th PERIOD

1159 - 1167

1113 - 1136

2nd PERIOD

1150 - 1159

5th PERIOD

1141 - 1150

1136 - 1141

4th PERIOD

3rd PERIOD

Seventh Period: 1167- 1179
Hildegard the Saint

- Hildegard founds a new abbey, Eibingen
- She falls ill again
- Hildegard heals the possessed woman
- Writes *Life of St. Disibod* and *Life of St. Rupert*
- Completes *Book of Divine Works*
- Hildegard's longtime confidant and secretary, Volmar, dies
- Hildegard has conflict with her new secretary, Guibert

- Prelates of Mainz impose interdict on Hildegard's abbey
- Interdict is lifted and Hildegard dies peacefully at age 81
- Hildegard proclaimed a saint by the people

Early Life

Hildegard of Bingen was born in the late summer of 1098 in a peaceful country estate located in Bermersheim, a town nestled in the lush Rhineland valley. Her parents, Hildebert of Gut Bermesheim and Mectild, were both from aristocratic families. Her father was a knight in the service of Count Meginhard of Sponheim in the castle of Beckelheim. Her mother was a member of a large and highly esteemed family of German nobility. Records report that as the tenth child in the family Hildegard was pledged as a tithe to the service of the Church.[2] Hildegard also had two brothers and a sister who eventually dedicated their lives to the Church. When she was eight years old, the little girl was taken to an anchorage attached to a Benedictine monastery near the Rhine River. In this enclosed dwelling for two or three women religious, she grew up.

There may have been other reasons for committing her to religious life so early. Since birth Hildegard had shown herself to be a frail child continually plagued with bouts of illness. Moreover, she exhibited strange behavior which proved embarrassing to the family. At the age of five, for instance, she frightened her nursemaid by accurately predicting the color of an unborn calf in a pregnant cow. Sometimes she claimed she could see faraway places or scenes from the past. With a childlike candor, she also spoke continually of regular appearances of a dazzling light which she could not identify but which somehow filled her with ecstatic joy.

Her parents may have thought her unfit for normal society and reasoned that a cloister away from the world would be a better milieu for this strange child. They knew that it was customary for convents to accept handicapped or socially ill-adapted daughters of the rich. Whatever the true reason for Hildegard's entering ordered religious life, it did prove to be a good environment for her. She was placed under the care of Jutta, who was a family acquaintance as well as a highborn anchoress from Sponheim.

We would probably find the rites for admission into the anchoritic life somewhat shocking today — especially for a child. The faithful would come to the church with lighted torches and recite prayers from the Mass of the Dead; the candidates for enclosure were expected to "die to the world" and spend their time in prayer before God. The bishop would bless the anchorites, and they would be locked behind the door for good. Jutta and Hildegard, along with a servant, lived in a small cottage next to the St. Disibod abbey church. None of them were allowed to see anyone except a confessor. Food was delivered through a door with a revolving hatch, and garbage would be sent out the same way. The anchorites were allowed one meal a day but because Hildegard was a child, she would be given two meals a day, one after three in the morning and another after three in the afternoon. Meals usually consisted of eggs, cheese, bread, fruit and vegetables, except on Sundays and feastdays when fish was allowed. Several times a day they went outside briefly to accommodate their bodily necessities.

During the day, Jutta taught the child rudimentary Latin suitable for church use, and trained her in the Benedictine traditions of music, spinning, biblical history and recitation of the psalter. Perhaps Hildegard also learned some craft, such as making combs or mats for the support of the monastery. Later she may have been taught more sophisticated skills. Some cloistered nuns did illuminations or were skilled in medicine and surgical techniques.

Hildegard always felt that her education was insufficient. She often referred to herself as an unlearned woman instructed only in simple letters. However, her writings show that she was acquainted with medical, philosophical, and biblical treatises. It is possible that she also received additional training from the monk Volmar, who became her lifelong friend, secretary and confidant.

We know little more about her younger days. Like other Benedictines, she devoted herself to prayer, silence, fasting, and work. Perhaps this contemplative routine served to develop in Hildegard a kind of interior reservoir of quiet, an inner spaciousness where she could receive the light more fully. She attended

Mass and sang the Divine Office eight times a day beginning with Matins at two in the morning and concluding with Compline in early evening. This everyday pattern must have provided a stable and rhythmic exposure to spiritual thoughts, music, and imagery. Such unyielding repetition could sink deeply into her psyche and stimulate her imagination.

Sometime between the ages of 15 and 18, Hildegard professed her virginity and received the Benedictine habit from Otto, bishop of Bamberg. By this time the anchorage had become a convent of nuns as Hildegard and Jutta's spirituality must have attracted more candidates to their way of life. Jutta was then appointed *magistra,* or administrator, of the small community.

Leadership and Vision

In 1136, at age 38, Hildegard succeeded Jutta as *magistra,* after the latter's death. Hildegard had about a dozen sisters under her charge at the Disibod convent. Within four years of her appointment, however, Hildegard's life changed dramatically. Without warning, a blazing light struck her. From within this shimmering aura, a voice spoke and issued a command that she speak and write all she learned in this audio-vision. The incident deeply disturbed her. She became very ill and fell into a state of depression. She who had kept silence about her extraordinary experiences for forty years was being asked to proclaim them publicly. Hildegard was caught in a dilemma. On one hand, she knew that holding in her experiences made her sick. On the other hand, expressing them seemed out of the question. She was just an unlettered woman, a weak instrument of God. Full of self-doubt and afraid of other people's opinions, she saw herself as a little person in the vast universe.

But something in her was faster and stronger than her fears and lack of self-confidence. Some Divine Wind was blowing, making marvelous music through the tiny trumpet of her person. Could she not just let herself be carried by the wind as easily as a feather on a soft breeze? To those inner voices that sought to delay or diminish her expression she admitted her weaknesses, but, like a good lawyer, she turned the tables. Could not her feminine fragility, a dominant concept in the Middle Ages, even become the basis for being a worthy channel for the Divine? Moreover, Scripture provided support. Didn't God's track record show the Divine choosing the weak to confound the strong? If so, then neither her gender, her meager schooling, her poor health, nor her personal insecurity could block her purpose. She would find a way. Her use of theology to overcome social obstacles is the first instance of a strategy we can recognize as distinctly Hildegardian.

Meanwhile, Hildegard had confided in her confessor, the monk Volmar, about these revelations. Volmar told his superior Abbot Kuno about her visions and it was through Abbot Kuno that word about Hildegard's visions reached Archbishop Henry of Mainz. Together with his theologians, the Archbishop examined the content of her revelations, proclaimed them as Divinely inspired and ordered her to begin recording them.

Feeling inadequate at polished writing, Hildegard decided to dictate her visions to Volmar whom she called her "file" because he "smoothed" her words so that they would have "a right sound for human ears." Hildegard usually wrote in Latin interspersed with some German, while Volmar assiduously refined the words of her revelations, putting them into correct Latin grammatical forms. Over the next 10 years, with Volmar as her secretary, she produced her first book, *Scivias* (Know the Ways), containing 26 visions, theological explanations, and a musical play considered the earliest known liturgical music drama written.

According to medieval standards, a certain systematic order of education was required in order to be considered learned. Hildegard knew that by these standards she was looked upon as uneducated. Furthermore, as a woman she was completely disqualified to present herself as a person with authority to write or preach. Although she firmly believed that the Divine command provided her with both the necessary authority and knowledge for the task, she realized she

I THE FIERY LIFE OF DIVINE WISDOM, SPARKLE THE WATERS I BURN IN THE SUN IN THE MOON AND THE STARS

would need a human support system if she expected to be taken seriously. She therefore sought and received confirmation for her revelations from the Church through her friend Abbot Bernard of Clairvaux. Again, we see an example of Hildegardian strategy. Bernard was a very influential and highly revered theologian of the day. The current pope was his protégé. Bernard spoke favorably about Hildegard to Pope Eugenius. He was then appointed by the pope to head a commission that would examine her work. Not long after, her writings received a stamp of approval from the pope and his bishops who were meeting at a synod in Trier.

By 1147, Hildegard had become something of a celebrity. Numerous young women flocked to enter the convent and the women's quarters at the monastery were becoming cramped. There were other problems as well. The nobility and the monks of Disibod were in constant conflict. The monks themselves were also becoming a source of irritation for Hildegard since she believed they were falling into lax habits. Moreover, they had claimed more and more of the monastery land for their exclusive use.

Hildegard petitioned her superior, Abbot Kuno, for permission to found a new convent on the mountain of St. Rupert near Bingen, a site revealed to her in a vision. The Abbot, persuaded by his monks and some of the nuns, resisted and denied her permission. Since Hildegard's notoriety had attracted many candidates to St. Disibod's and increased its endowments, her presence had proved valuable and profitable to the monastery. The monks were reluctant to lose the benefits. Hildegard, therefore, called upon her strength as God's oracle and let the Abbot know what awaited him should he persist in blocking the will of God. She also did not hesitate to use human assertion, calling her superior a "bungling ass." The abbot still refused and Hildegard fell ill again. Alarmed at her condition and fearful of Divine repercussion, Abbot Kuno relented and gave his permission. Remarkably, she immediately regained her health and proceeded with her plans to move.

Unwilling to endure the hardships the new situation would surely entail, several of the sisters at Disibod refused to leave. To add to Hildegard's difficulties, Sister Rikkarda, her spiritual protégé and second secretary, left to accept the position of abbess at another monastery. Rikkarda also happened to be a cousin of Jutta and daughter of the Marchioness von Stade who was a generous benefactor to Hildegard. Hildegard had developed an affectionate attachment toward Rikkarda and her departure was one of the saddest experiences in her life. Although Rikkarda later relented and decided to rejoin Hildegard at the new convent, she became ill and died before she was able to come back. Hildegard was deeply affected by this loss.

By 1150, Hildegard had transferred about 50 sisters and their dowries to the new foundation. Hildegard had not only procured the new convent but had also gained legal and financial independence from Abbot Kuno. She recognized only the Archbishop of Mainz as her superior and secured imperial protection from Frederick Barbarossa for her monastery. With the financial help of her friend the Marchioness von Stade, Hildegard built her new convent on the grounds of a dilapidated monastery. It was designed according to Hildegard's specifications with large, beautiful rooms and workshops furnished with the modern convenience of piped water. This installation of a water system shows Hildegard's interest in and knowledge of the new science of engineering. She was probably also aware of the mechanical conveniences, such as water-powered machines for milling and automatic flour sifters, which Abbot Bernard had ordered for the remodeling of his monastery in Clairvaux.

In 1165 Hildegard founded a second convent at Eibingen and thereafter spent her days commuting between the sites twice a week. Sometimes, as she commuted the eight miles by boat, Hildegard would take time to cure people who came to the shore for help, using Rhine water as a sacramental.

The establishment of the new monasteries was an important step for Hildegard. It provided her with what historian Sara Evans calls "free space" — the psychological conditions ideal for the full flowering of Hildegard's awesome gifts.[3]   We could perhaps name the ingredients of this free space: freedom from woman's domestic and reproductive role, financial independence, room to exercise her authority, and a supportive environment for her creative endeavors.

At both Rupertsberg and Eibingen, Hildegard created communities of women who had the rare opportunities to develop intellectual, artistic, and spiritual gifts under her leadership. On work days, the sisters kept busy in the workshops weaving cloth, copying books, doing artwork, or performing other manual labor. On feast days, they would practice reading and singing. The sisters sang freshly composed music, kept a wholesome schedule and maintained a healthful diet. Apparently, they also made use of Hildegard's remedies which included warm mineral baths, exercise and rest. Hildegard advocated drinking beer in place of the often polluted water and claimed it provided weight gain and rosy cheeks.

In the style of a good administrator, Hildegard allowed a certain measure of expressive freedom among her nuns. As virgins — brides of the Lamb — these women celebrated holy days by wearing white veils, tiaras with gems, and putting rings on their fingers. When another Rhineland abbess criticized Hildegard for the fancy clothing her nuns wore, she responded that it was women's place to "flash and radiate" Divine beauty. She also reminded the abbess that the monastic virgin had a right to adorn herself beyond the secular matron because it was done out of love for the heavenly bridegroom. In this example, Hildegard reveals her attitude toward the human body, particularly, the female body. She did not view it as an object or even solely as an instrument of service. For Hildegard the body seemed more like a sensitive and poetic expression of the soul. As such it could be decorated, beautified and finely clothed to reflect the radiance of the inner spirit.

The two monasteries were rich in piety as well as income, yet we know that community life in the two convents was not idyllic. Just as in any other human situation, there were conflicts, jealousies and power struggles among these daughters of the wealthy class. At least once, Hildegard refers to having to endure the "glowering eyes" of her sisters.

Creativity and Medicine

Hildegard's own creativity flourished in the years after her move to Rupertsberg. She completed her trilogy of prophetic-symbolic writings: *Scivias* (Know the Ways), *Liber Vitae Meritorium* (Book of Life's Rewards), and *De Operatione Dei* (Book of Divine Works). *Scivias* also contained 26 colorful and sometimes startling illustrations which were completed under her supervision in the convent scriptorium. Meanwhile, she carried on a large correspondence with a wide spectrum of people who sought her counsel. Among the people who wrote to her for advice and admonition were King Henry II of England and the German Emperor, Frederick Barbarossa.

The oddest of her creations seems to be her *Lingua Ignota,* a secret language consisting of 900 nouns and 23 alphabetical letters. She may have invented these words for her own diversion, for medical purposes, to create a mystical bond among her sisters, or for a purely sensorial effect since she employs them in some of her hymns.

Hildegard was probably the first German scientist and medical doctor. She produced scientific books based on her own observations of nature including stars, plants, trees, herbs, animals, rocks and gems. Her encyclopedic medical compendiums contained over two thousand remedies and health suggestions including experiments with folk healing. Some of Hildegard's health tenets included the idea that the body, like the cosmos, was an organized energy system which needed to be kept in balance. The four dynamic elements to be maintained in equilibrium were moisture, dryness, heat and cold. Hildegard also believed that all illnesses could be reversed except asthma and migraine which were more stubborn. There are indications that Hildegard herself may have suffered from these illnesses. She also taught that the four principles of good health were rest (freedom from stress), a balanced diet, exercise and a moral life.

Her interest in medicine moved Hildegard to a practical compassion and treatment for women's difficulties. She was one of the few known healers who commented on gynecology and obstetrics. Most medieval physicians would not accept women as patients so they could "concentrate their efforts on the worthy sex."[4] Hildegard scholar Barbara Newman writes about various remedies prescribed by Hildegard for women. These included herbal baths for menstrual pain and the use of precious gems together with incantations for infertility. She even had a special potion for women to use to keep from being harassed by unwanted lovers! Newman remarks that Hildegard's orthodoxy prevented her from including medical helps for abortion, birth control, or feigning virginity.[5]

I AM THE RAIN

COMING FROM
THE DEW THAT CAUSES
THE GRASSES
TO LAUGH WITH THE
JOY OF LIFE.

Hildegard's Music

Hildegard was also a composer and her music is one of her most priceless gifts to us. Her works number over 60 antiphons, sequences, hymns, and responses for the liturgical year. In addition, she wrote the first musical drama, which she called the *Ordo Virtutum* (Play of the Virtues). Scholar-musician Barbara Thornton comments that this work may have been written to celebrate Hildegard's new Rupertsberg foundation with 15 of the 50 women there singing the role of the virtues, and Volmar, the only male present, taking the spoken part of the devil.[6]

Hildegard's songs are strikingly beautiful, original, and perhaps eccentric compared to what we know as the mainstream style of composing in her day. While most medieval Gregorian chants are smooth and narrow in scope, Hildegard's chants are leaping melodies with a larger pitch range of two and one-half octaves. Rather than using metric strophic forms with repeated music at each stanza in her hymns, she allows her music to follow the thought imagery and word accent more freely, and she even interjects highly decorative melodic passages.

With her typical flair for grand organization, Hildegard compiled her musical works into a liturgical cycle which she named *Symphonia Harmoniae Caelestium Revelationum* (Symphony of the Harmony of Heavenly Revelations). She was one of two composers of the medieval period to attempt the completion of a work of such large dimensions. The other was Peter Abelard.

Music had an important symbolic value for Hildegard. She believed that it recreated the original harmony that existed between God and humanity in the garden of Eden. For her, each human heart was a resonant and receptive instrument from which God could draw beautiful tones as from a lyre. The devil, on the other hand, envied humankind's resonance with God and sought to steal this harmony. He lived in the place of no-music, had no capacity to sing, and spoke in a shrill, cackling voice.

The word "symphonia," or symphony, had a special meaning for Hildegard. Living in symphony meant living a life of virtue in tune with the harmonious praises of the nine choirs of angels in paradise. Such a life would be inspired, filled with Divine purpose, and so powerful that everything would work together for the person in a harmonious way. Contemporary poet, Jessica Powers describes this kind of graceful living in her poem "Indwelling":

> I walk in a cloud of angels
> I move encircled by light and glowing faces
> . . . Stricken by music too sublime to bear.[7]

According to Hildegard, this vibrant mandala of singing angels would be the normal environment for the human being — what God wishes for each of us. Being in symphony could not be achieved by any means except by profound desire and the bounty of God.

Today we know that many women were active as musicians and composers before Hildegard. Her immediate predecessors known to us were Hrotswitha, a tenth-century German Benedictine nun from Gandersheim who composed poetry, drama and music; and Kassia, a Byzantine nun in the early ninth century who wrote about 49 liturgical compositions. Unfortunately, Hildegard was not aware of these women composers who preceded her. As Gerda Lerner explains in *The Creation of Feminist Consciousness*, women's lives and works were not included in mainstream history written by men.

In Hildegard's day, music was a subject in the higher order of medieval education called the Quadrivium. The other subjects were astronomy, geometry and mathematics, but usually only highborn males received this kind of education. Generally, women were considered incapable of abstract thinking. Hildegard claims that she composed music without any formal training. Nevertheless, hearing and singing liturgical songs for eight sessions of Divine Office each day must have seeded her musical imagination.

Theology: The Feminine Divine

Hildegard was the first important person in the middle ages to talk about religious experience in terms of feminine archetypes.[8] Her theological writings, song-poetry and iconography are filled with an impressive array of feminine figures and images. These images well up from her poetic genius influenced by familiarity with Scripture, medieval readings, her surrounding Rhineland geography and her own experience as a woman. A large number of her illustrations are designed using forms associated with the feminine such as circles, curves, waves and ovals. In the third vision in *Scivias*, for example, Hildegard pictures the universe as a cosmic egg where God, humanity and nature lead an interrelated, interdependent life.

The immediate sources of her images, however, were the intense stream of audio-visionary experiences which began when she was forty-three years old. Everything she saw and heard appeared within the non-spatial light that Hildegard called "The Living Light" or sometimes "Reflections of the Living Light." Within this shimmering brightness there appeared colorful, dynamic feminine figures of staggering power and beauty. In her theological trilogy, *Scivias*, *The Book of Divine Works* and *The Book of Life's Merits*, Hildegard reveals to us her vision of a colossal salvific drama in which these feminine figures played important and essential roles.

The first forceful, feminine, divine, figure we meet in Hildegard's panorama of salvation history is the godlike figure of Sapientia — Divine Wisdom personified. Divine Wisdom as a female persona of God has long roots in tradition. Hildegard was certainly familiar with Her appearances as Hokmah in the Book of Proverbs, and in the deuterocanonical books of Baruch, Ecclesiasticus, and the Wisdom of Solomon. In several of these instances, Wisdom praises Herself in the style of a goddess. For example, in Proverbs 8, Wisdom says of Herself:

> I, Wisdom, give good advice . . . Because of my strength, kings
> reign in power, unending riches, honor, justice are mine to distrib-
> ute . . . From ages past, I am.

Hildegard's Sapientia, or Lady Wisdom, first appears in the fourth vision of her *Scivias* where she represents God's providence and foreknowledge. Hildegard does not hesitate to describe Her in a divine splendor which embraces both tenderness and strength:

> This figure was shining so brightly that I was not able to see her
> face nor the garments that she was wearing . . . She is as terrible in
> regard to fear as lightning is menacing, and she is as soft in regard
> to goodness as the sun is bright.[9]

This image does not stereotype feminine qualities as simply soft, sweet, and passive. Rather, Hildegard associates the feminine divine with "menacing strength" as well as "soft goodness." In the illustration, Lady Wisdom is presented as a Divine Presence with aspects of a pre-Christian nature goddess. Sometimes she even wears the same stylized crown as the ancient Near East goddesses.

Hildegard dresses Lady Wisdom in the rich clothing of nobility in the ninth vision:

> Her head was radiating like lightning . . . She was clothed with a
> tunic of a gold color . . . She wore a girdle which descended from
> her breast right down to her feet. This girdle was embellished
> with gems and was decorated with shining purple-colored glitter-
> ing, but the girdle was green, white, red, and the color of air,
> blue.[10]

In this vision, we see a glimpse of Hildegard's appreciation of beauty and the high value she placed on the aesthetic in life. Here she again links woman with beauty and with culturally valued commodities such as jewels and fine apparel. Hildegard herself had a taste for rich garments and felt free to allow her sisters in community to don fine clothing on feastdays.

Hildegard again affirms women by associating motherhood with divine creativity in another image of Lady Wisdom which she presented in a hymn, "O Virtus Sapientiae." Lady Wisdom is the Matrix of being, the Creatrix in whom the earth dwells as a child in the mother's womb. She is not a distant prime mover; rather she "looks into the world for people," for she "loves people greatly [and] protects [them] with her own protection." As creatrix-mother she enfolds the universe in her wings and envelops it in her circular odyssey of the earth:

> O moving force of Wisdom, encircling the wheel of the cosmos, encompassing all that is, all that has life in one vast circle. . . .[11]

The encircling, encompassing movement seems to suggest a womb-like image.

A second feminine divine figure enters into Hildegard's God imagery. Caritas, Lady Love, is also a Wisdom figure like Sapientia but with slightly different nuances. Hildegard writes, "Wisdom and Love are one." We might think of Her as an alter ego of Sapientia. Her emblems are the deer who thirsts for God (Psalm 42) and the mirror, which in Hildegard's symbology signifies heavenly desire and the splendor of Divine Beauty. In a dazzling canticle, Hildegard the visionary portrays Caritas in the imagery of fire and as God's "helpmate" dancing in the symphony of creation, recalling earlier concepts of goddesses as Divine Consort:

> O burning light of the stars, O most splendid model of the regal nuptials, O glowing jewel! You are arrayed as a high-ranking woman with neither stain or fault. And you are the playmate of the angels, a companion to the holy ones.[12]

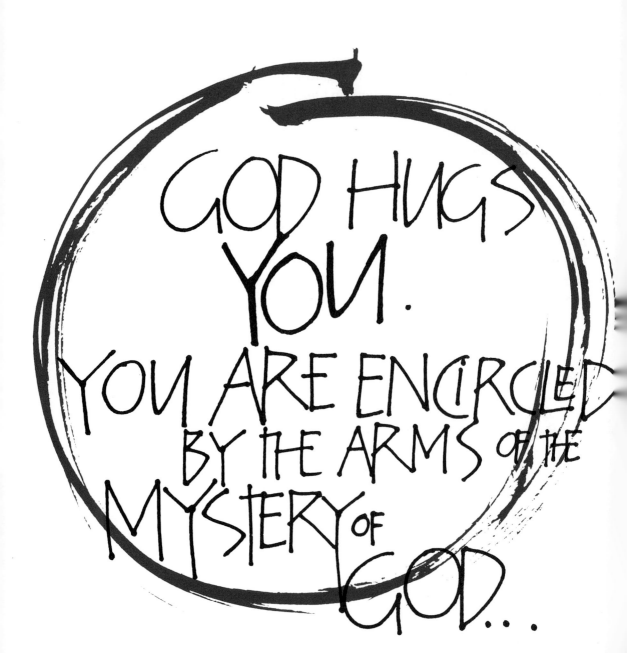

Elsewhere, Hildegard associates Caritas with the goddess Natura — the *élan vital* or elemental force that invigorates nature. Her golden light glows in each of us and all creation sparkles with her radiance and beauty. In the first vision of *Scivias*, Hildegard speaks for Caritas:

> I am life, whole and entire . . . All life has its roots in me . . . All life lights up out of me. I am life that remains ever the same, without end. For this life is God, who always is in motion and constantly in action.[13]

Lady Love glows with "viriditas" — the vigor of love that "hugs the world: warming, moistening, firming, greening [it]." She is the " flame [that] nourished the clod [of earth] (Adam), just as a mother nurses her child . . . and a person was brought forth."[14] Again, we see Hildegard affirm women's bodily experiences as holy and pertaining to divine behavior. Implicitly, she is also validating another female symbol — the earth and its resources. Hildegard must have been thinking of her beloved Rhineland valley where the lush green earth was visited with frequent rainfalls.

Mary, Ecclesia and Eve

A third figure in Hildegard's array of feminine divine images is a woman who mirrors Lady Wisdom's eternal counsels and brings Her visions to fulfillment — Mary the Mother of God. For Hildegard, Mary is the historical figure who unites the celestial and earthly. She is the reflection of Lady Wisdom — the Divine spinner who meshes divinity and humanity in her eternal weaving of life. For Hildegard, Mary, too, is a spinner who reveals women's true role: to birth the divine into the world.

As a human being, Mary also mirrors Eve, the mother of humankind, who foreshadowed Mary's role in God's plan for human salvation. Hildegard believed that every woman who gave birth was a spinner of God-flesh, clothing God with humanity and thus conquering the serpent. She thought that Satan was sterile and envied women who in bearing children were constantly reminding him of God's birth into the world through Mary. Hildegard was probably the first person to record the idea of womb envy. In her medical book, *Causes and Cures*, Hildegard advises women at childbirth to use demon repellents such as jasmine and fern fronds because the devil lay in ambush for every child. Hildegard's explanation gave the reason for the many crib deaths in her day, while her ritual-remedy provided a psycho-spiritual armor for mother and child.

Mary, Virgin-Mother, was (and still is) an ambivalent symbol. By giving birth and remaining a virgin, she is an impossible model for women. Moreover, it seems that her authority derives in secondary manner by way of association with her Son. For Hildegard the issue is unresolved as well. In typical Hildegardian strategy, she tries to explain away the first objection by saying that woman before the Fall would have been capable of giving birth without violating her virginity. Hildegard also believed that in paradise the sexual act would have resembled the action of light passing through a stained-glass window. Curiously, she does not remove passion from this notion. We can see this in her hymns to Mary, which preserve what Barbara Newman calls "a gentle eroticism." A text from one of Hildegard's chants conveys this idea:

> Your flesh has known delight like the grass land touched by dew
> and immersed in freshness.[15]

In regard to Mary's divine status, Hildegard wavers between her image of Mary as Mother of God and Mary as Mother God. For example, in Hildegard's *Symphonia* (Dendermonde manuscript), Mary's chants occupy a central space between chants devoted to God the Father and those dedicated to the Holy Spirit. We might assume that momentarily Hildegard's Mary replaces the Son/Christ as the middle member of the Trinity. However, to solve her quandary about Mary's divine status, Hildegard evolved a different theological rationale for this placement. In her view, the Mother-and-Son formed an unbreakable combination, so in Hildegard's thinking Mary could rightfully occupy this space within the celestial trinity.

Another sign of Hildegard's struggle to validate the feminine divine shows up in the type of imagery with which she constantly surrounds the Virgin. Musician Barbara Grant, in an article on Hildegard's songs to the Virgin, remarks that Hildegard presents the Virgin as a composite of elements of Isis, the Egyptian goddess, Demeter, the Greek goddess, and Aurora, the Roman goddess of the dawn.[16] In a characteristic overlay of images, Mary assumes symbols reflecting not only Lady Wisdom but those of Lady Love as well. She is the Bride of God. This leads Hildegard to draw connections between Mary and the Church personified as the woman figure, Ecclesia. Hildegard sings,"now let the sunrise of joy be over all Ecclesia and let it resound in music for the sweetest Virgin Mary. . . ."[17]

Both Ecclesia and Mary have cause to make music and to dance because both give birth to the "Song" of God, the Word. In fact, music seems to be an emblem for both Mary and Ecclesia. Hildegard often associates music with divine presence and with women. Women, like music, had the power to weave heaven and earth together into a harmonic unity. This association explains Hildegard's extreme anger and frustration when her convent was placed under interdict and her nuns were silenced for a period of time. In her eyes, this interdict not only brought a demonic element into her convent but it also suppressed the exercise of sacred feminine power.

Powerful as she is, Ecclesia nevertheless becomes another ambivalent figure in Hildegard's roster of feminine archetypes. In using a woman figure to represent the Church, Hildegard again puts herself in a problematic position. Given medieval notions of women as the inferior sex, she virtually "feminizes" the church and finds herself using the negative side of the metaphor in her symbolic development. Ecclesia as Bride is subject to her Divine Husband, Christ. She is obedient to His will. In articulating these ideas, Hildegard is caught in confirming the domination-subordination model so familiar to women's experiences. On the other hand, Hildegard again turns the image around to help her accomplish her goals. If Ecclesia is subject to Christ, then clerics too must show the womanly virtue of obedience because they represent Ecclesia. Frequently, Hildegard made use of the Ecclesia figure as her strongest mouthpiece for reprimanding priests and teaching them attitudes of humility.

As the feminine divine becomes enfleshed in the faces of real women, the problem of the legitimacy of female power becomes more crucial and more of a struggle for Hildegard. In the discussion of flesh and blood women, she reveals the strongest tension in her thought. It is as if she brings her personal struggle to the fore and asks us to participate in its solution. Eve seems to be the crux of her tension.

Eve, like Lady Wisdom, is a theophany. Like Mary, she is archetypal mother. Yet Eve succumbs to Lucifer. Instinctively, Hildegard resists Augustine's theory that Eve was to blame, *in toto*. Given her resplendent theology of Lady Wisdom, how could she believe that Eve-woman was not also a house of wisdom? Hildegard grapples with her problem in her strange pictorial representation of the Fall. Here she portrays Eve as a green cloud (a very unusual symbol of a person even in medieval iconography). The cloud emanates from the side of Adam and is filled with stars. To one side the serpent spews a dark venom over the cloud. Incidentally, Hildegard treats the serpent symbol with a great deal of respect. She lived close to the forest where there were still many vestiges of religions which associated the snake with the feminine. She says that the devil chose the snake to represent himself not because it is cold, venomous and sneaky but because it was the least demonic and most trusted of the animal world.[18]

Woman's Cloud Nature and Sexuality

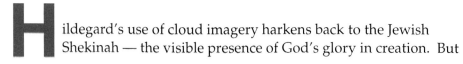

Hildegard's use of cloud imagery harkens back to the Jewish Shekinah — the visible presence of God's glory in creation. But the cloud also had an immediate meaning for Hildegard. In medieval biological typology, woman was considered to be made up of elements from water and ether (a substance lighter than air). Thus women were considered more "airy," permeable, and open.

Hildegard stretches this notion further to signify that woman was spacious, inspired, able to shelter stars within herself. Unlike man who was made from the clods of earth and was therefore stony, hairy and stubborn, woman was made from flesh and therefore of finer material. Hildegard's keen appreciation of woman's body reminds me of poet Adrienne Rich's description:

> She is beautiful in ways we have almost forgotten . . . Her body possesses mass, interior depth, rest and balance.[19]

However, Hildegard immediately inverts her image. Woman's cloud-like nature also makes her more vulnerable, more susceptible to illness and evil persuasion. Hildegard believed that she herself suffered many illnesses because her body was fragile, "airy" and open to diseases that floated in the air. In fact, to this day the noxious Rhineland winds do cause allergies to many residents of the area.

Shifting to the other side Hildegard becomes Eve's defense counsel. If Eve succumbed to evil, it was not due to willfulness or obstinacy but because her elemental softness was susceptible to harm. She was violated by Satan. She was victimized by him and was not capable of resisting. In Hildegard's theology, Eve never seduced Adam; he simply caught Satan's illness by contagion.

Hildegard did not fully subscribe to Augustine's theory that lustful desire was the root and punishment of original sin. While she believed that lust was sinful and that sexuality would have been less equivocal without the Fall, she thought that the punishment for original sin lay in menstrual pain and labor pangs. At the same time, in Hildegard's theology, these things related to woman's main purpose — clothing God with flesh, giving birth — so woman's condition was occasion for both mercy and judgment.

Assuming a scientist's mentality, Hildegard saw sexuality as natural and as a symbol of the union of God and humanity. She took a stand against the Cathars who preached that carnality even in marital relations was suspect. Unlike the common opinion of the day, Hildegard believed that woman's cloud nature actually made her less sensual and more spiritually inclined than men. Her medical works show that she sympathized with woman's reproductive role and knew what a source of anxiety it was to her secular sisters.

Her widest departure from the medical opinions of her day regarding women is her idea that unless the woman experiences orgasm, there will be no conception. She believed that the woman, too, emitted a seed, but only when aroused. In a rather bizarre theory in which she compared the process of conception to the making of strong cheese, Hildegard taught that only love expressed by both parties during intercourse would produce a wholesome child.

Hildegard believed in the complementarity of the sexes. Theologian Rosemary Radford Ruether would perhaps describe her as a "romantic feminist." Man depended on woman for his "robe of flesh," and woman depended on man for his protection and support. Her notion of complementarity also included the idea that men, too, suffered biological repercussions from the Fall. While woman suffered menstrual discomfort and labor pains, man's sperm became contaminated and his noxious sperm tainted human conception. However, the female womb and blood, which Hildegard considered holy, could neutralize this contamination and have benign effects on the fetus.

In the Middle Ages a bleeding person, especially a bleeding woman, could not go into a church because blood was something that could profane a sacred place. But as far as Hildegard is concerned, a menstruating woman could enter the church because her blood related to life; a wounded soldier, however, could not enter the church because his blood related to the taking of life.

TO A WORLD
TORN BY
FRENZIED
VIOLENCE,
HILDEGARD
BRINGS HER VIEW OF A
UNIVERSE
ALIVE WITH
DIVINE WISDOM AND
LOVE.

— FIERRO

Creative Authority through the Feminine Divine

As we can see, an ambivalent strand ran through Hildegard's theological thinking about women. On the one hand, she exalted the feminine as divine and associated her with Eternal Wisdom and creation. On the other hand, she valued the feminine as holy primarily because of association with the male-imaged God-Ruler and his Son. While Hildegard apparently could not solve this theological problem in an intellectual way, she did resolve it through her visions and their empowering effect on her life.

Oliver Sachs, a medical expert on the nervous system and author of the book *Awakenings*, studied Hildegard's visions carefully as they are illustrated in her works. He discovered a strong similarity between her drawings and the various visual phenomena described by patients suffering from severe migraine headaches. He says it is not unusual for migraine sufferers to experience "dramatic disturbances" in the visual field. They see twinkling brilliancies and auras that are often invested with "great rapturous intensity." He further comments that the migraine sufferer is often one whose nervous system is trying to find a way out of an insoluble problem. In the process, he believes that this unresolved tension creates visual phenomena in an effort to view the world in a new way.

Dr. Sachs feels that Hildegard suffered from serious migraine headaches and that her migrainous visions, "burning with profound theophorous and philosophic significance," offered a physiological ground for the Divine to direct and inspire her to a life of mysticism.[20] He believes that her deep mind yielded the transforming symbols she needed. I would add that one of these symbols was possibly an internal archetypal image of a deified feminine figure that could affirm feminine values, attributes and qualities.

Perhaps it was Hildegard's scientific-spiritual comprehension of God as Vital Reproductive Power or her sense of the sacred as all-embracing that disposed her to encounter the feminine divine. Whether the basis was psycho-physiological, intellectual or strictly revelatory, is hard to know. What we do know is that Hildegard began to conceive of God in a new way, imaging the divine in forms which could also exalt woman's goodness, generativity, creativity, imagination, aesthetics, style of intelligence, self-confidence, strength, bodily processes, spirituality and compassion. This original theological perspective had a great impact on her own psychology.

Far from the pale and passive way women are often pictured, the invigorating feminine figures Hildegard saw were "brilliant as the sun" with creative authority to "enkindle the moon, enliven the waters and awaken everything to life."[21] Such a radiant divine femininity could empower Hildegard because in it she discovered a mirror of her self and a way to access her own power and possibility. Hildegard's investment in God as also feminine in gender provided the strong inner template she needed to counter the inferior and debilitating images of the feminine foisted on womankind by society's biased myth of female inferiority. I believe that in this deified symbol of feminine authority she found her own depth and her significance in the unfolding events of history.

It is not surprising, then, that in 1158 Hildegard broke all precedents by preaching in public. Emperor Frederic Barbarossa invited the "Sibyl of the Rhine," now 60 years of age, to undertake four missionary tours to further the cause of Gregorian reform. Despite a bout of severe illness, Hildegard went on her preaching journeys, making visits to over 21 cities and acting as a trouble shooter at monastic chapter houses. The successive tours took place in 1160, 1161-63, with a final journey in 1170, when Hildegard was 72 years old. Some of her preaching is preserved in correspondence to clerics and prelates who asked for copies of her sermons. We have to admire the courage and stamina of this older woman who, against all social expectations, dared to travel over a 200-mile radius by foot, litter, horse or boat exposing herself to brigands, thugs or thieves who always lay in ambush for unsuspecting travelers.

Last Years

In 1169, Hildegard had a frightening encounter with a possessed woman from Cologne. The woman, Sigewize, had reportedly been plagued by a devil for eight years. Though she had visited numerous shrines of saints with friends who attempted to help her, nothing could be done for her cure. Sigewize finally approached the monks at the Brauweiler monastery, but neither were they able to help her. The evil spirit also insisted that only the "old woman further up the Rhine," whom he derisively referred to as "Scrumpilgard" (Wrinklegard), could heal her.[22]

As it was not in a woman's province to perform an exorcism, Hildegard created a theatric ritual involving seven priests to cleanse the woman. When this failed to alleviate her problems in a permanent way, an appeal went directly to Hildegard. Though reluctant to do so, she invited Sigewize to live in the convent under her ministration. The woman's erratic behavior disturbed and frightened the nuns, but eventually her spirit seemed to calm in the peaceful and prayerful atmosphere of the monastery. Then during the Holy Thursday ceremonies at the convent, the devil suddenly departed, causing the woman to have an embarrassing bowel discharge in the middle of the assembly. The woman was sent home completely cured.

In the last years before her death in 1179, Hildegard experienced a severe hardship. After Volmar's death, two men were pressed into Hildegard's service as secretaries: first, the monk Gottfried, who also took the opportunity to begin writing Hildegard's *Vita*, then Hildegard's own brother, Hugo. Meanwhile, she invited Guibert of Gembloux, a Belgian monk, to visit her Rupertsberg monastery. Guibert, a highly educated man fluent in many languages, had taken great interest in her work. So when a fever took the lives of both Gottfried and Hugo,

Guibert became Hildegard's last secretary. Unfortunately, he took it upon himself to edit Hildegard's dictated words according to his fancy. This of course irritated her, and for several years there is evidence that friction existed between the two. Guibert was a great admirer of Hildegard's achievements. More likely it was his overzealous desire to perfect her work rather than his ego that prompted him to the unorthodox editing. Guibert remained with Hildegard during her difficult times and, after her death, he wrote down her life story. A fragment of his *Vita Sanctae Hildegardis* manuscript still exists.

At the age of 80, Hildegard faced her most difficult trial. She had given permission for a revolutionary youth to be buried in the monastery grounds. Since the youth had been excommunicated, Hildegard's immediate superiors, the prelates temporarily in charge while Archbishop Christian was away, demanded that she exhume the body from consecrated ground. The elderly abbess appealed to the prelates, making a special trip to present her case to them in person. But the prelates remained adamant about their position and ordered her to proceed with the removal of the corpse. She refused, claiming that she had definitive proof that the young man had confessed and been anointed. But the prelates continued to be deaf to her pleas. With feelings of bitterness and sadness, Hildegard returned home and sought counsel in the Living Light.

Receiving divine confirmation for her position, the feisty abbess went to the cemetery, blessed the grave with her abbatial staff and deliberately removed all traces of the burial so that the body could not be found. As a result, the prelates placed her convent under Church interdict. This meant that Hildegard and her nuns could not have Mass celebrated, receive Communion, or sing the Divine Office — an occasion of public shame for the cloister. Hildegard complied with the interdict but wrote a firm letter to the prelates appealing for a restoration of liturgical privileges. In her letter she gives an eloquent explanation of the salvific significance of music in the divine plan. She also tries to intimidate her superiors by casting doubt on the sincerity of their motives and by warning them that those who silence God's praises on earth would find themselves consigned to a place of no-music, where Satan himself resided.

This situation caused great agony for Hildegard, particularly since she believed that music was a vital link between God and humanity. The interdict would also have prevented Hildegard from receiving the last rite of anointing — a fearful threat for an aging abbess since this anointing was considered a necessary and final preparation for entry of the soul into heaven.

The problem dragged on for months as the Archbishop of Mainz was still absent. Hildegard summoned her strength and wrote a letter to Christian asking him to review the proof she had of the rightness of her decision and to lift the interdict. With reinforcement from Philip, the Archbishop of Cologne, Hildegard's plea was eventually heard. Soon after, in March of 1179, the interdict was lifted. Spiritually and physically exhausted, Hildegard died peacefully on September 17, 1179.

There are no detailed records of Hildegard's final moments, but legend reports that at her death the skies lit up with colorful lights. She was immediately accepted as a saint by popular veneration, even though official canonization was held up by administrative red tape and, in fact, never completed. Nevertheless, her name appeared in the Christian calendar of saints in the fifteenth century. Her relics lie in Rudesheim near the Rhine river while her heart and tongue are preserved in a church reliquary at Eibingen where her monastery, the Abbey of St. Hildegard, still thrives today.

Epilogue

Hildegard's writings were well known during her lifetime and were modestly circulated for sometime afterwards up until the mid-sixteenth century. With the coming of Scholasticism, the Reformation and the Age of Rationalism, however, her ideas gradually fell out of favor. Moreover, her life and work were not accorded the importance that her male counterparts enjoyed. Women's creative work has repeatedly been obliterated or marginalized by historians.

Today, knowledge of Hildegard's life, her music, and her spirituality is spreading. The women's movement of the seventies sparked keen interest in women's artistic and intellectual accomplishments, and this launched a reclamation of women's cultural contributions. Hildegard's stunning works are among many accomplishments by women which have recently emerged from the shadows of history.

There is a deeper reason, however, for Hildegard's emergence now. She has come to us because we need her. There is a thirst for the kind of balanced and colorful spirituality that she provides. To a world torn by frenzied violence and annihilation, she brings her fresh view of a regenerative, cooperative universe alive with Divine Wisdom and Love. Her words rekindle a belief in the value and importance of each person's role in the unfolding cosmic drama. For women, in particular, Hildegard brings hope by showing us a vision of the Divine that affirms us as women — our bodies, our minds, our hearts and our powers.

In her comments on Hildegard, historian Gerda Lerner draws our attention to the significance of the little motif Hildegard often paints in the corner of her icons. Lerner says that this self-conscious logo may be the first of its kind for a woman.[23] Hildegard was no longer just God's tiny trumpet but a whirlwind woman claiming her gifts. She pictures herself seated and alert, with her face uplifted, radiant and alive. From this place, she seems to admonish us once again: **"Do not be afraid. You, too, have visions, passions, dreams. Claim them!"**

Endnotes

1. Connie Zweig, "The Conscious Feminine: Birth of a New Archetype" in *Mirror of the Self*, ed. by Christine Downing (Los Angeles: Jeremy Tarcher, 1991), 183.

2. This information can be found in Gottfried of St. Disibod's *Vita Sanctae Hildegardis*.

3. As quoted by Gerda Lerner in *The Creation of Feminist Consciousness from Middle Ages to 1870* (New York: Oxford University Press, 1993), 58.

4. Bernard W. Scoltz, "Hildegard of Bingen on the Nature of Woman," in *The American Benedictine Review*, 31 (1980), 377.

5. Barbara Newman, *Sister Wisdom* (Berkeley: Univ. of California Press, 1987), 152..

6. *Hildegard von Bingen: Ordo Virtutum*, Sequentia (77051-2-RG, Harmonia Mundi). Barbara Thornton, liner notes.

7. Robert F. Morneau, *Mantras from a Poet: Jessica Powers* (Kansas City: Sheed & Ward, 1991), 105.

8. From a videotape interview with Barbara Newman: *Hildegard of Bingen* (Washington Cathedral, 1989). Rev. Canon Leonard Freeman, executive producer.

9. Hildegard: *Scivias*, trans. Bruce Hozeski (Santa Fe: Bear and Co., 1986), 216.

10. *Scivias*, 312.

11. Hildegard: *Book of Divine Works*, ed. Matthew Fox, trans. Robert Cunningham (Santa Fe: Bear and Co., 1987), 368.

12. *BODW*, 393.

13. *SC*, 11.

14. *SC*, 80.

15. Text trans. from liner notes on recording *Sequences and Hymns by Hildegard of Bingen* (London: Hyperion Records Ltd.).

16. Barbara L. Grant, "Five Liturgical Songs by Hildegard of Bingen" in *Signs*: *Journal of Women in Culture and Society*, 5 (1980), 559.

17. Hyperion liner notes.

18. This interpretation of Hildegard's attitude toward the serpent is based on Bruce Hozseski's translation. The Hart translation differs in interpretation.

19. As quoted in Nelle Morton's *The Journey Home* (Boston: Beacon Press, 1978), 169.

20. Oliver Sachs, *Migraine: Understanding a Common Disorder* (Berkeley: Univ. of California Press 1985), 106.

21. *BODW*, 11.

22. Sabina Flanagan, *Hildegard of Bingen: A Visionary Life* (New York: Routledge, 1989).

23. Lerner, 64.

Annotated Bibliography

Books by Hildegard:

Scivias (Know the Ways). Santa Fe: Bear and Co., 1987. Trans. by Bruce Hozeski.

Scivias. New York: Paulist Press, 1990. Trans. by Columbia Hart and Jane Bishop. Contains insightful and scholarly preface by Caroline Walker Bynum and introduction by Barbara Newman.

De Operatione Dei (Book of Divine Works), Santa Fe: Bear and Co., 1986. Trans. by Robert Cunningham. Edited by Matthew Fox Both translations are excellent. I would recommend starting with secondary sources before reading these books. In this translation inclusive language replaces Hildegard's words. While the reading becomes more palatable because c this, we can lose the flavor of the medieval framework which does in fact encase Hildegard's otherwise startling thinking.

The Book of the Rewards of Life (Liber Vitae Meritorium). New York and London: Garland Publishing, Inc., 1994. Trans. by Bruce Hozeski.

Hildegard von Bingen Lieder. Salzburg: Otto Muller Verlag, 1969. Edited by Pudentiana Barth O.S.B., M. Immaculata Ritscher, O.S.B. and Joseph Schmidt-Gorg.

Saint Hildegard of Bingen: Symphonia, Ithaca/London: Cornell University Press, 1988. Introduction, translation and commentary by Barbara Newman.

Books about Hildegard:

Fiona Bowie and Oliver Davies, *Hildegard of Bingen: Mystical Writings,* New

York: Crossroads, 1990. A good basic book summarizing Hildegard's life, times and teachings.

Gloria Durka, *Praying with Hildegard of Bingen.* Minnesota: St. Mary's Press, 1991.

Sabina Flanagan, *Hildegard of Bingen: A Visionary Life.* New York: Routledge, 1989. A more scholarly and detailed approach to Hildegard's life and works. Excellent follow-up to Bowie's book.

Matthew Fox, O.P., *Illuminations of Hildegard of Bingen.* Santa Fe: Bear and Co., 1985. Beautiful photo reproductions of Hildegard's vision-illustrations. Includes Fox's inspiring ideas and research on them.

Barbara Lachman, *The Journal of Hildegard of Bingen.* New York: Bell Tower, 1993. A fictional and imaginative diary of one year in Hildegard's life (from Advent 1151 to Epiphany 1153).

Barbara Newman, *Sister Wisdom.* Berkeley: University of California Press, 1987. A splendid exposition of Hildegard's ideas on the Feminine Divine aspects of God.

Carolyn Sur, *The Feminine Images of God in the Visions of Saint Hildegard of Bingen's "Scivias."* Lewiston, New York: Edwin Mellen Press, 1992. This is a publication of Dr. Sur's thesis. Includes some color prints of Hildegard's icons.

Gabriel Uhlein, *Meditations with Hildegard of Bingen.* Sante Fe: Bear and Co., 1983. Both Durka and Uhlein's books are good, devotional approaches to Hildegard's spirituality.

Drs. Wighard Strehlow and Gottfried Hertzka, *Hildegard of Bingen's Medicine.* Santa Fe: Bear and Co., 1988. These physicians update Hildegard's medical language so that we can make practical use of her remedies.

Ingeborg Ulrich, *Hildegard of Bingen: Mystic, Healer, Companion of the Angels.* Trans. by Linda M. Maloney. Minnesota: The Liturgical Press, 1990. A poetic, fictional biography of Hildegard.

Articles on Hildegard:

Jan D. Bent, "Hildegard von Bingen," *The New Grove Dictionary of Music and Musicians.* Sixth edition, edited by Stanley Sadie. London: Macmillan, 1980. (Vol. 8. 553-556).

Barbara L. Grant, "Five Liturgical Songs by Hildegard von Bingen (1098-1179)," in *Signs: Journal of Women in Culture and Society,* 5 (1980), 557-567.

Bruce W. Hozeski, "Hildegard von Bingen's Ordo Virtutum: The Earliest Morality Play," in *The American Benedictine Review,* 26 (1975), 251-259.

Bernard W. Scholtz, "Hildegard of Bingen on the Nature of Woman," in *The Benedictine Review,* 31 (1980), 377.

Selected Discography

Recordings:
There are numerous recordings of Hildegard's music now being issued. The most scholarly, authentic, and creative interpretations come from the Sequentia ensemble.

"Abbess Hildegard of Bingen: A Feather on the Breath of God." Sequences and Hymns. Gothic Voices. Hyperion A66039.

"Hildegard von Bingen: Ordo Virtutum." Sequentia. Two disc set 77051-2-RG Harmonia Mundi. Remarkable rendition of Hildegard's medieval opera.

"Hildegard von Bingen: Symphoniae." Spiritual songs. Sequentia. Deutsche Harmonia Mundi 77020-4RG.

"Hildegard's Chants." Elektra Women's Choir. Skylark 9202.

"Columba Aspexit." Gothic Voices. Hyperion 66227

"Hildegard von Bingen." Music composed by Hildegard and arranged for medieval instruments and synthesizers by Vladimir Ivanoff. Vox Diadema 343.

"Hildegard's Lauds of St. Ursula." Focus 911. Indiana University Press Recording.

Videotape on Hildegard:

"Hildegard of Bingen." Washington Cathedral, 1989. Executive producer, Rev. Canon Leonard Freeman. Morehouse Publishing Co., Harrisburg, Pennsylvania. A beautiful and inspiring presentation of Hildegard's life and thought through interviews of people who have researched, reflected and love Hildegard and her contributions. Accompanied by a booklet with suggestions for group discussions of ideas presented. One hour in length.

Acknowledgement:

Hildegard's illustrated quotations are reprinted from *Meditations with Hildegard*, by Gabriele Uhlein, Copyright 1983, Bear and Co., P.O. Box 2860, Santa Fe, NM 87504.

Nancy Fierro, CSJ is a noted concert pianist and lecturer. She has recorded four commercial albums and presented recitals in the United States, Canada, Mexico and France. An authority on music by women, Dr. Fierro has published numerous articles on women composers and she lectures regularly for the Los Angeles Philharmonic at the Music Center. Her work has won several awards including the Sigma Alpha Iota Radio-Television Award, A Certificate of Honor from the International Congress on Women in Music, and a California Arts Council Touring Artist grant.

Nancy earned a Doctor of Music in piano with secondary areas in music history and feminist theology from the Univesity of Southern California. She also received a Certificate in Music from the American School of Fine Arts in France. Currently, Dr. Fierro is on the piano faculty at Mount St. Mary's College in Los Angeles.

Madaleva Williams, CSJ is a well-known graphic artist. After studying with Corita Kent in Los Angeles, she became an art educator and is now active as an artist-in-residence at the Center for Spiritual Development in Orange, California where a variety of her work is on display.